SCRAPBOOK

ISBN   978-0-578-71969-6

Cover Photo Steven Bradley Carter

Editors
Ann Sallemi
Barbara Agte

Bluwaters Press
www.bluwaterspress.com
Deming, NM 88030

Books by BETTE L. WATERS

Memoir
Curves, Points, and Hair

Poetry
My Daddy Brought Me Up To Be Good

Health Issues
Massage During Pregnancy Editions 1- 4
So, You're Pregnant
Ask A Midwife
My Mother Was a Spaceship, Monologue

Autobiography
Dream Boat Cruising, 33 Dangerous Days
My Mother Was a Spaceship
Ask A Midwife

Oral History
Blue Eyed Country Boy: IW Local 387
Beef Jerky Muscle on Barbed Wire Bones
Vaginal Politics

PUBLISHED BY BLUWATERS PRESS[1]

How Did That Get In There?, Twana Sparks. M.D.
Through The Left Eye of James Sander-Cederlof, autobiography
You Can't Put God In A Box, Sherri McClellan Moseley
Confusing My Tenses, Ann Sallemi
The Mousetrap, Ann Sallemi
Under Cover, Under Fire, Jose Quintero
Making My Way, Charles McClellan
Thirteen Weeks, An Anthology of Screen Plays
Wayfarers: The Spiritual Journeys of Nicholas & Helena Roerick,
Drayer
Vaginal Politics, A Midwife Story, Judy Lee
One Foot Away From A Million, Don E. McCoy
To The Sea Again, Billy McClellan
Children of the Big Sioux, Paul Bringman
Kent Letters, Students Response to Kent State Massacre, 1970, Agte
The Last Cattledrive, Thurston Comstock
Autopsy of the Soul, Maria Reynolds
Whoa, You Donkey, Whoa!, Laura Leveque
El Perdido, The Lost One, Randy G. McGowan

---

[1] Copies of the books listed above are available from Lightning Source, Ingram Content Group. Tennessee, USA. Or any local bookstore will order individual copies.

TABLE OF CONTENTS

CHAPTER ONE

Vincent Louvenia Grooms

February 25, 1879 – June 9, 1961
Wesley Chapel Cemetery, Alma, Ga. [2]

My grandmother, Vincent Louvenia Grooms, born and raised in South Georgia was a force to be reckoned with. She was a strong woman long before any living female today was referred to as being a feminist. For the purposes of brevity, I am choosing to refer to Vincent Louvenia Grooms, Waters, Henderson, as Grandmother.

She is also listed in some internet-finds as Vincie Lorrine Grooms. Both entries of the spelling list her as having been born in Tattnall County Georgia. Reidsville, its county seat, is famous because the Georgia State Prison is located there. In my childhood the town name was synonymous with the prison. As a child anyone known as having been sent to jail was described as "sent to Reidsville".

I called her Grannie. It was a name she did not care for; she corrected me uncountable times for calling her Grannie. As a child, I understood that as Grand- mother, the mother of my daddy, she was an

---

[2] These dates taken from records of The Church of Jesus Christ, Latter Day Saints genealogy records (Mormon Church.)

important person. Her relatives referred to her as Vinnie. No one referred to her as being crippled. Yet she was physically crippled.

Preparing to write this biography I contacted all the cousins I could find asking for family stories. Some of the cousins remembered that our grandmother's crippling was a result of some field accident when she was a child, but they had no memory of how that story began within their family group. Because there is a lack of agreement among cousins about our grandmother's physical injury that left her a cripple, I am choosing to use my memory of the story.

As a young child grandmother jumped from a farm wagon to the ground and injured her knee. In today's world the most common injury to the knee is a torn cartilage referred to as the meniscus. Using my education received from the Medical University South Carolina, I am presuming this was a torn meniscus, a very painful injury.

The most comfortable position was keeping her knee bent approximately at a thirty-degree angle with no weight bearing on it. When the injury was healed, the pain gone, her knee was frozen at this angle. As an adult, the only activity this injury ruled out for her was working as a field hand. Knowing how she lived her life as an adult, I'm sure that she put all her efforts into walking on the ball of her foot and playing in the yard as a skinny child, it is obvious that she certainly had a fairly normal adulthood as a young woman.

Grandmother could read and write. Supposedly, she could read and write and cipher at a time when schools teaching these subjects were free. However, in the deep south, free education was dependent on the local tax base of each county, meaning free education was a long time coming. I never heard her speak about any type of formal education.

Vinnie, as her family called her, married as a young woman to Henry Shelton Waters. I found a Henry Shelton Waters who died in 1956 in Bacon County.

I can only guess that a separation with a legal divorce was way above anyone's pay level in these times. Yet, it was known by some members of our family, that a married man by the name of Williams sired her two sons, Troy and Elmer, and a daughter Grace. These children went by the surname of Waters. Later, she married Harley Henderson, and gave birth to R. H. named Richard Harley after his father. Their last child was named Singey, a girl, who in today's world would have been considered mildly retarded. It was my under-standing that as an adult my father knew who his father was, but they never had any interactions as far as I knew or garnered in any research.

I discussed the above information at length with my siblings and cousins, attempting to come to some comfortable decision about the telling of this portion of her history. Some relatives approved, but most of them did not. I am choosing to rely on the advice of my long-time friend, Janet Sipple, and editor of every book I have written, Ann Sallemi. They both remind me that biographies are for telling the truth.

It is interesting that when I was a young child my grandmother scolded me for something I had said, or some speech pattern I used, telling me that I sounded like "Gullah/Geechee". She did not describe what sounding like a Gullah/Geechee was, but she led me to believe that to sound like a Gullah was not a good thing. How could she know about the Gullah who lived on islands sixty miles east—islands at the time, with no bridges to the mainland. I never knew about the Gullahs until recently when I learned that Judge Clarence Thomas was born in Pin Point, Georgia, an unincorporated Gullah community on the coast.

In 1938, all grandmother's children were grown and married, and some returned to her home after divorce, bringing young children and new partners with them. I was one of those young children. In 1938 her son, my father, Perry Elmer Waters brought his three children to his mother's home from a farm owned by his father-in-law two counties over. She took us in. My sister, a six-months old baby, was farmed out to the care of my father's newly married sister Grace. My brother, Raymond and I lived with Daddy and Grandmother at 818 E. 11th Avenue, Alma, Georgia.

It was a shotgun house, long and narrow with a front porch, a great room, containing three double beds, a back door with a step down to a porch. A smaller room off to the left was the kitchen. The cooking device was a woodstove. The kitchen had a long table, with benches on each side, and wooden chairs at each end.

10

Close to the back porch was an open well. We had to draw water out of the well by hand with a bucket attached to a chain that rolled along a grooved wheel hanging mid-center over the well opening. The curb of the well was approximately waist high to the adults.

In the back yard was a small shed with dirt floor where Grandpa Henderson lived. He was Grandmother's husband, but they did not live together. The shed had one small wooden window, and the floor was made of wooden boards lying on top of dirt. Grandpa took his meals with my grandmother. I called him Grandpa; but in reality, he was not my grandfather.

There was an outdoor toilet on the very edge of her back yard.

I can only speculate about how my grandmother came to own this house.

CHAPTER TWO

Grandmother's visit

My first memory of my grandmother was before I was old enough to go to school. She came for a short stay. During this time, mama and daddy had a dance at our house. They moved the beds into a small side room leaving only a few chairs in the main room of the house. That night I was placed in the side room with my brother and sister who were sleeping. Daddy and mama were members of the local Mormon Church that believed in having music and dancing. Several musicians showed up, and what seemed to me a large gathering of people. The guests spent maybe an hour of time shelling peanuts to be stored for spring planting, and then the instruments came out and dancing began.

Mama put me and my brother and sister in the side room where one bed from the big room was set up for use. Mama came in to check on us. My siblings were sleeping; but, I was wide awake, excited by the music and smells.

Mama gasps out loud and grabs our farm cat that was in the basket containing six newborn kittens. The local tomcat had chewed off the heads of every one of the kittens. Mama scolded me and pushed me away from the window ledge where she was holding the basket. But I saw them anyway. I don't remember that I was sad or hurt. I was curious not frightened, due to not under- standing what the tomcat had done.

At this time I was not yet old enough for school attendance. During that visit Grandmother and Mama took the Sears Roebuck catalog pages and sewed scraps of cotton cloth across a paper page, trimming the edges, making squares for a patchwork quilt. The squares were finished, but before they would be sewed together to make the quilt top, the paper had to be torn off the backside of each square by hand. I was good at that. And felt like I was helping.

The quilt patches and its lining would be stretched out tightly onto quilting sticks— long boards with holes bored along its length to hold the sides of a quilt. They would have the quilt material on ropes hanging from the ceiling. When ready to actually work the hand stitching of the quilt, they lowered it to a comfortable height allowing the quilter to sit in a chair while quilting. When it came time to make supper, or perform other duties around the house, the women would wind the string on the quilt strips raising the large square toward the ceiling where their work hung out of the way until next day's quilting time. And then my grandmother was gone.

CHAPTER THREE

Mama

The morning of mama's disappearance Daddy woke me, "Do you know where your mama is?" he said. I followed him into the kitchen where he showed me the warm ashes in the stove, "She made food," he said. "She's gone." At age six, I was too young to understand the gravity of my mother's leaving.

A few days later, getting off the school bus at the gate of our farm, walking down our long lane toward the house, I saw two women who wore long beautiful dresses—strangers to me. Daddy's sister Aunt Grace and Grandmother had come to help.

Several days later, Grandmother and Aunt Grace were gone taking my sister and brother with them. Daddy did not own the farm. He was working as a sharecropper for his father-in-law, Judge Edward Hood.

My Uncle Melvin Hood—mama's brother—had returned from out west where he had been working for the WPA. Daddy and Uncle were on the front porch smoking Prince Albert roll-your-own cigarettes.

Earlier that summer Daddy had purchased with precious pennies a small carnival-glass bowl from a peddler who stopped at our house. The peddler had sold it to him, harking it as unbreakable. To demonstrate it being unbreakable the peddler slung the bowl across the long front porch striking the wood floor several times and bouncing off the edge landing neatly on the soft ground with no damage.

Daddy was demonstrating for Uncle Melvin the unbreakable glass bowl. He gave it a sling across the porch in the same manner as the salesman a week or so ago. It hit the porch a couple of times landed on the edge of a board and split into two pieces. Daddy, swearing, picked up the pieces while Uncle Melvin tried to hold in laughter. I had witnessed the peddler perform this demonstration and I was surprised, too. Of course, it would be years before I would be mature enough to appreciate the behavior of my dad and his grace of living the life of a poor sharecropper, the farm belonging to his father-in-law, my grandpa.

That summer and early fall, me and Daddy stayed on the farm for the harvest of the late crops, like corn. That done, we joined my brother and sister, who were in the care of daddy's mother and sister in my grandmother's home located in Alma, Georgia.

CHAPTER FOUR

WPA

At the time, under the order of our President Franklin Delano Roosevelt the Works Progression Administration was established. This definition comes from the Works Progress Administration (WPA); renamed in 1939 as the Works Projects Administration and was an American New Deal Agency, employing millions of jobseekers (mostly unskilled men) to carry out public works projects, including the construction of public buildings and roads.

By 1930, the Great Depression had plunged the United States into economic chaos as stock prices plummeted, banks failed at alarming rates, unemployment reached record numbers affecting nearly every American family. Elected President in 1932, Franklin D. Roosevelt with his team created a series of program and reforms known as the New Deal intended to achieve economic recovery and to provide relief to the millions of poor and unemployed.

The Federal Emergency Relief Act (FERA) allowed the Federal Government to assume partial responsibility for relief available to the workers. In 1935, this New Deal was expanded to include the Works Progress Administration.

This new organization, the WPA, was made for the honest, efficient, speedy, and coordinated execution of a work relief program and to move workers from the rolls of relief to work. Originally, it was for moving persons from the relief rolls to production work on public projects or private employment. All, for the head of the household, the husband, the father, in other words the male.

Upon the insistence of First Lady Eleanor Roosevelt, a women's division was created within the WPA. Part of this program was the WPA Sewing Project.[3] The women's division projects also included housekeeping, and care of the sick.

The sewing room project was one of the more popular programs for women. On November 1, 1935, the program began with the goal of furnishing garments for sale, and to offer employment to unskilled women who needed to work for a living. In order to qualify for one of the jobs, the woman had to be the head of a household, have the potential to hold down a job, be unemployed. Women who had husbands able to work did not qualify.

Grandmother, at least in her early fifties, met all the criteria. At the time she enrolled in the sewing project, she had a husband, Harley Henderson. I was never able to find any records of their legal marriage. At the time, he was physically unable to work and dependent on my grandmother. At some time, he

---

[3] The Sewing-Room Projects of the Works Progress Administration, Sara B. Marcketti, Textile History, 41 ((I).28-49, May 2010

had signed up on the county rolls as poor and needy, and received a small stipend of a few dollars a month.

He lived in the small shack out back that had boards laying on dirt for a floor. It contained a double bed, a huge trunk, and a shelf hanging over the head of the bed. There was an 8 x 10 framed black and white photo of Grandpa sitting in the back of a two-seater biplane. As a child, I was impressed when Grandpa said he flew it. Uncle R.H. (his son) pooh poohed this, saying Grandpa paid someone to take a photo of him sitting in the pilot's seat.

In addition to lying to his grandchildren, he chewed tobacco, paid to have the Savannah Morning News delivered daily, helped with gardening and always kept a sweet potato bed over the winter that contributed to the kitchen coffers.

He grew the potatoes in the garden he tended, hired someone to plow them up. We kids piled them in a mountain hill. He placed a thick layer of pine needles over them and covered everything with dirt to protect them from the winter frost. Thanks to his work we would have baked sweet potatoes every day.

Grandpa sat on Grandmother's front porch in a rocker. He walked around the house to take his meals in her kitchen, but I never saw him enter the big room of her shotgun house. Practically every day, he walked uptown—maybe a two-mile round trip.

Just across the dirt street of the house was a deep cut. In fact, it was referred to as 'the cut'. It was maybe 80-90 feet wide and ten to twelve feet deep as it allowed the railroad tracks to move through Alma avoiding a hill—saving the railroad company money on coal fuel. The cut went through the town and was probably the deepest where a concrete bridge crossed it carrying the famous US Highway One. At the southwest corner of the bridge was the Alma Hotel.

At the time daddy moved us from the farm after mama left, grandmother was leaving the house several days a week. A couple houses from her shotgun on the north side of the cut there was a set of wooden stairs that led down into the cut. On the other side across the tracks was another set of steps that allowed one to climb out of the cut on the south side. Grandmother walked to her job using these steps to cross the railroad track, which saved her many steps on her daily trek by foot. I had no awareness that she had a job. I knew that several days a week, she made this trip on foot.

I am taking a leap here, and presuming she was attending sewing classes organized and taught by the WPA Sewing-Room project. It is not clear if grandmother attended classes to learn how to sew, resulting in the items mounted in her scrapbook, or if she was required to demonstrate that she had sewing knowledge. The other important part of the Sewing Room was the students got paid a small stipend to attend. Proof positive of her pride in her accomplishment, she placed the samples of her sewing in the scrapbook. And over the years, every female in our family that ever saw the scrapbook admired it; and many coveted the scrapbook. I know I did.

The scrapbook has nineteen pages. Each page shows a sample of stitches, hems, flocking, gathers, sleeves, collars, buttonholes, demonstrating her class work, except for the last page. Written on the bottom of the empty page is one word, bonnet. She had no access to glue, so she stitched the examples of her work onto each page. Each page has on the front the example of sewing stitches and on the back are tight threads that hold the sample onto the page. The pages are yellowed, aged and fragile. Best I can cipher, the pages and sewing samples mounted onto them, have to be at least 80 years old.

Over the years every family female that ever saw her scrapbook coveted the missing bonnet. In my memory it was three by four inches in size and would have fit on the average baby doll head. It was made of unbleached cotton material, and identically matches what is referred to today as a "trek bonnet". In my research, never was there a clue as to who took the bonnet. My only concession is to say, it had to be a female thief, men would have had no interest in her sewing skills.

An attempt to identify information about the WPA Sewing Room and where it might have been located in Alma results in Dottie Ray's letter from The Historical Center of Alma/Bacon County, Georgia.

"Dear Ms. Waters,

We have not been very lucky finding much information on the WPA in Alma, Georgia. I did find History of the Alma/Bacon County Public Library that might be of some interest to you. This letter was from the WPA of Georgia.

August 31, 1940, an agreement was reached between officials in Bacon County and the Works Projects Administration (WPA) to participate in the Library Project. The City of Alma, the County Board of Education, and the County Commission each agreed to pay $10.00 ($30.00 total) monthly to buy new books.

The City of Alma was represented by Mayor M. E. Jones; the Board of Education by the school superintendent, Mrs. E. C. Perkins; and the Bacon County Commission chairman, J. W. Douglas.

The Alma Times, Thursday, November 30, 1933, 196 Jobs Given to Alma and Bacon County $1,764 Weekly Payroll to be Continued Through January. One hundred and Ninety-six jobs have been given to Bacon CountyCitizens by the emergency relief corporation, it was announced here today. The work, which consists mainly of street and drainage improvement work will be continued at least through January 1934. An average salary of nine dollars per week is being paid the men.

CHAPTER FIVE

Where do babies come from?

Summer of 1938, Daddy with me and my brother Raymond lived in Alma, Georgia with his mother Vincent Louvenia Grooms Waters Henderson. My sister, Robbie, was a baby not yet walking, and living with Daddy's sister, Aunt Grace and her new husband.

A young teenager, related to the family via some kind of marriage situation, came to Grandmother's home to play with me. We were in the yard, and she introduced the subject of where baby's come from. She explained to me about babies in our mother's bellies and how they might get out. I listened, as we played marbles and other dirt games.

However, that night, I took my sister's doll to bed with me. Assuming I had privacy under the covers that night, I took the doll and placed it between my legs above my knees, trying to imagine how a baby could come out of a woman's belly.

Suddenly my grandmother was at my bedside, jerking the sheet off me and exposing the doll I had placed between my legs. "What are you doing?" She exclaimed as she picked up the doll. I was more surprised at her interest than I was embarrassed. Looking at this event today, I did not have enough information to be embarrassed. I had no ideas of sex stuff, nor that baby stuff was part of sex stuff, and was totally unaware of any adult protections set up to keep my innocence intact.

This event was never spoken of between us.

CHAPTER SIX

The Alma Hotel

When I decided to write about our grandmother, I sent a communique' to cousins, uncles, aunts asking for stories and photos. One of the best responses comes from second cousin Diane Ricketson.

Her dad Earl was more like a brother than my cousin. Below is Diane's response, which set me off on a journey I had not anticipated—the hairy search for proof of relatives living for months on end at the Alma Hotel.

Grandmother's daughter, Grace
met and married a Ricketson in Millwood, Georgia. Grace and her husband lived with Grandmother Henderson for a short while. Grandmother's son-in-law could find no work in the Alma area, and they moved to Akron, Ohio, where he went to work for Firestone Tire and Rubber Company.

I seriously questioned the story that our grandmother lived at the Alma Hotel, or that her daughter, Grace, had lived there because her estranged husband paid her child support.

The country was in the throes of the Great Depression and who would have had the money to live at the Alma Hotel. However, the hourly wages paid by Firestone in 1937 ranged from $0.77 for

Janitors to $1.11 for machinists. The highest hourly pay was Electrician $1.15.[4] This was great pay and was indicative of what labor unions were seeking, beginning with a first Firestone contract negotiation in 1937.

Grace had two boys with this man; but due to marital problems moved back to Alma to live with her mother, my grandmother. Due to child support payments, they supposedly, along with Grandmother, occupied the upstairs far back left room of the Alma Hotel. They stayed for several years. Grace met her second husband through a friend and married him in May of 1939.

I found registered at the Clerk's office in Bacon County a Quitclaim deed release from her son, Troy Waters for her shotgun house, dated in 1939. Thus, I am certain she did not live at the Alma Hotel. So, there is paper proof that in 1939 our grandmother owned the shotgun house on 11th street that overlooked the railroad cut.

---

[4] Wage Chronology, Firestone Tire and Rubber Company (Akron - Plants) 1937-66; United States Department of Labor, Bureau of Labor Statistics; Bulletin No. 1484.

CHAPTER SEVEN

Grandmother's Shotgun House
and Mosquitos

It is not clear how my grandmother came to own this shotgun house, built on one 25 foot by 90 foot lot. Although there is a registered Quitclaim deed at the Bacon County Clerk's office signed by her son, Troy Waters, dated in 1938 relinquishing the property to his mother, in 1938 Troy was married and lived in Statesboro, Georgia, with his family.

The two lots west of the house were empty. No one claimed this property and grandmother used the space for planting a spring and fall vegetable garden. The house was the typical front porch, a big room, a step-down to a porch at the back with a side room off the porch that served as a kitchen. The step-down back porch did not have a roof.

The kitchen had one window that opened outward, as did the windows in the big room—all windows were wooden slats with no glass. There were no screens on any windows or doors to protect us humans from mosquitoes.

On summer nights to protect against mosquitoes for sleeping, grandmother used a tin coffee can, placed loosely a hand full of cotton from the local farmers fields. She would light a small piece of paper and stuff it into the cotton in the tin. The cotton would smolder at length producing a heavy whitish smoke. Maybe a half hour before everyone's early bedtime, grandmother would lit this smoke can, leave it in the big room with the beds and we would rest on the front porch waiting for the smoke to drive all the mosquitoes out of the house. When completed grandmother would place a glass dish over the top of the can smothering any spark; we would go to bed free from any discomfort of biting insects interrupting sleep.

CHAPTER EIGHT

Snuff

Over the months of writing this missile, and my brain searching for memories of Grandmother, the subject of tobacco use surfaced. Growing up in South Georgia, all the older females used snuff. The males chewed tobacco. Even Grandmother's tight-ass religious sister, Mary Ann, used snuff. Back then churches taught that smoking was a sin.

When I asked my 28 year second cousin, who lives in south Georgia, to tell me what he knew about snuff, he does not know what I am talking about. When I explain, "Ground up tobacco," he replies, "Oh, you mean dipping."

He explains his dipping days, and his preference brand of Silver Topped Copenhagen, long cut—long cut because, "...it irritates the gum and you get a faster physical reaction to the nicotine."

Way more information than I expected. Yet, happy to hear that he no longer dipped. I forgot to ask if he smoked. Of course, smoking is supposedly more sanitary than dipping, yet dipping keeps the foreign stuff out of the lungs.

In the decades of our grandmother's younger womanhood, it became socially hip to smoke cigarettes, especially if you were female. Of course, men had been using tobacco for centuries. In fact, documented tobacco growing began in this country

when it was less than 200 years old.   A colonist, John
Rolfe from Jamestown, arrived in Virginia with
tobacco seeds procured on an earlier voyage to
Trinidad and harvested his first crop in 1612.

Our grandmother did not use tobacco in any
of its forms. In fact, the most frequent argument she
had with her husband, Harley Henderson, was his
chewing tobacco on the front porch and spitting,
most times missing his mark the yard, and his spittle
spattering on the edge of the porch floor. It disgusted
her, but he just ignored her and continued his nasty
habit. Possibly one of the reasons he slept in the one
room shed out back.

CHAPTER NINE

Soap Making

The recipe for home-made soap from lye and animal fat was in Grandmother's head. It was a combination of water, old rank animal fat, or crackling made from unwanted animal parts at butchering time, and a can of lye. She would eyeball her mixing of ingredients stirring it in a large cast iron pot in the backyard. She would build a fire under the short legs of the pot, as the water reached the correct heat, she would add each ingredient. Then for some amount of time, she would stir and adjust the heat, and stir. As a child, I wanted to stir, but she did not allow us kids to get involved—this being potent stuff cooking. I remember some superstition associated with which direction one stirred the soap concoction. You were to stir left to right. If you changed directions of the stir, the soap would not harden when it cooled. I don't know that anyone ever tested that directive.

The great thing about the soap, it worked really good on work clothes that could have any imaginations of dirt embedded. She never needed bleach, because of the strength of the soap. If you were not careful while using the metal scrub board used for extra dirty clothes, the soap would damage knuckles.

The soap was also used in the kitchen for dishwashing. Again, the soap, not so easy on the hands, but it killed germs on dishes and kitchen tools.

Out of curiosity, I searched the internet for lye soap. There are recipes and people everywhere who still make lye soap. I am delighted to see the custom has not floundered in this space age; although, when Grandmother made soap, it was necessary, not just a hobby.

CHAPTER TEN

Daughters-in-law

Grandmother had a sister known as Aunt Mary Ann. Aunt Mary Ann was married, religious, barren, and an overall tight ass. Mary Ann owned a house a block away from grandmother, and grandmother rented it out for her. It was the usual two-room house, front room large in order to fill with beds, and the back room smaller with a chimney for a wood cook stove.

In 1937, it was rented by "Shine" Tanner. Shine was a sharecropper who had grown too old to farm. Over the years, he had been known to make a bit of moonshine to support his family. He had three grown daughters at the time; two of his daughters were still single and living at home.

Grandmother, his landlord, had daddy and my single uncle R.H. living in her shotgun house. These two men began dating Shine's two daughters. Soon, grandmother had two new daughters-in-law and I had a stepmother. R.H. took his bride Pearl off to live uptown. Daddy brought his new wife, Lola, to his mother's shotgun house. Circumstances wrought with trouble.

U. S. Highway One went north and south right through Alma, Georgia. The small towns, along its path through South Georgia, had gas stations with ropes lined along U.S. Highway One where chenille bedspreads for sale were displayed.

Daddy was working at a local sawmill, living on 11th Street with Grandmother, me, my brother and sister. Before meeting his bride-to-be, he had purchased one of those chenille bedspreads as a present to his mother. It was not fancy just one large flower pedal outlined with colorful chenille stitching.

Grandmother's shotgun house had the one big room where three double beds were set up. Daddy and my new mama slept in one bed, me and my brother and sister slept in one bed, and then there was Grandmother's bed.

Grandmother was very particular about her bed. It had a top mattress that was made of feathers. Each day she shook out the feather bed and carefully smoothed the sheets with the bedspread on top. No one was allowed to sit on her bed during the day.

Her new daughter-in-law coveted that bedspread. Since my dad, her husband, had paid for it, she felt she had some rights to its ownership. I am not sure if there was ever any discussion between the two women about whose bed it should be used on.

It is late afternoon, all of the family except daddy who is at work, are in the back yard. Lola comes out of the house smoking a cigarette; she tells me to go in the house and get a chair. I am a bit slow in my obeying, and she yells at me, "Do what I told you!"

I step into the back door where grandmother's bed is the closest to the door. The bedspread on her bed is on fire beginning near the floor. I scream and run back "Fire, fire!" Everyone comes running. Lola gets there first. She grabs the spread off the bed and throws it out the nearby window that just happened to be open.

Grandmother's spread is ruined; Lola must have accidently set the fire when she lit her cigarette; aren't we all so lucky that the house did not burn down. The bitch! She could not have the spread, so she destroyed it. Back then, I knew in my bones, it was purposely destroyed and now I can say it. Decades later, remnants of this chenille spread were in my grandmother's chest at the time of her death.

CHAPTER ELEVEN

WWII with Grandmother

World War II broke out in 1942; and at some time Daddy moved us to Jacksonville where he worked in a shipyard, leaving Grandmother to her own resources. The war ended in September 2, 1945, and it was not long before Daddy was laid off. No war, no need for ships. We returned to Alma, Georgia, to the shotgun house of Grandmother. I am not sure how WW II impacted grandmother's life, but Uncle R.H, her youngest son, served in the United States Navy; and, he did not return home for some months after the war officially ended.

Daddy needed a job. No one seemed to be hiring. At age 12, I was out of pocket, so to speak, in that I had nothing to read; no way to go to the library, so I read the newspapers. Grandpa Henderson subscribed to the Savannah Morning News, a daily paper. Someone in the family subscribed to The Alma Times, a local weekly. No comics page, but I read it anyway.

This particular week there was one job listed on the classified page. It was a listing at a local service station located on Highway One and sold gasoline.

Daddy is heading out the door for his daily job search, and I told him about the job advertised in the paper. He did not believe me. I had to find the paper and show him the advertisement. Daddy took the page with the advertisement and left. He returned later in the day with the job.

This eased a lot of tension swirling around in Grandmother's shotgun house, especially for me. My stepmother did not care for me, and I actually hated her. I tried not to let my real feelings show. She did not attempt to hide her disdain for me, her smart-ass stepdaughter, who strongly disapproved of her and her alcoholism.

By this time in her life, my stepmother was clearly a full-blown alcoholic. She would order groceries from the main grocer in town. The store would fill the order and then send them to our house delivered by a driver in a truck. My step-mother had a deal with the delivery man that he would stop by the liquor store and buy her a pint of whiskey, put it in with the groceries and charge it to Daddy's running credit at the grocery story. How she drew him into her alcoholic scheme is up for anyone's imagination. I have always believed she paid him with sex. She had no money, how else could she have gotten him to help her commit this kind of stealing.

For years Daddy could not figure out why he was never able to pay off his running bill at the grocery store.

Uncle R. H. returned from the Navy, and got himself hired by the local rural electric association. After some months of his working there, he got Daddy a job at the same place. All this time we are living under Grandmother's roof. Daddy and his wife, my stepmother, convinced Grandmother she should let Daddy tear down her house and build a large four-bedroom with an indoor toilet.

He built the outside walls and the roof, but the only room inside that had a wall was the bathroom, that for a long time only had a commode, no sink or tub. Grandmother's bedroom had one wall that separated it from the kitchen area.

We lived pretty much this way until I left home at age seventeen to marry. I was not privy to the dynamics of the household, but my stepmother and Grandmother had a big row, and Grandmother rented a bedroom from a neighbor lady, Miss Taylor, who lived two doors down.

Here she is, displaced from her own property, and her youngest son, R.H. returns home from service in the Navy. Who knows what took place between the two brothers; yet, Daddy purchased a vacant lot around the corner. Daddy and his brother, my Uncle R.H., built my grandmother a house located on the corner of Wayne and Eleventh Streets. It had two bedrooms and a kitchen with an electric stove. The bathroom only had a sink and a commode, but their mother, my grandmother, owned a home and it was paid for.

No way to know how many family members found our grandmother's home a sanctuary. I know I was one. I lived with her for several months when I was pregnant with my second child. My husband worked out of town. She cared for me when I came home with my newborn, giving me one of the best gifts of my life, making my breakfast every morning. I was breastfeeding, and sleep was always intermittent. The waking up to bacon, eggs, hot biscuits was, for me, the depth of luxury. I was not an ungrateful young woman, but it never occurred to me to share with Grandmother what a gift she was giving me. When she died, my dad Elmer, and my sister Olidia were living with her.

CHAPTER TWELVE

Baby Dolls

We were living in Grandmother's shotgun house, and mama came to visit. It was the first time I saw her after she left me, Daddy and my siblings at the farm. She was alone and driving a dark green Buick sedan car. She gathered me and my brother, Raymond, taking us to a motel on the outskirts of Waycross, Georgia.

My youngest sister, Robbie, Mama's baby was in the care of Aunt Grace who lived on a farm several miles away. Waycross was maybe thirty miles south of Alma. Not sure why Mama did not find accommodations in Alma. She took me and Raymond for overnight and bought us jodhpur pants, along with some other clothes. I don't exactly remember them as jodhpur pants, but I remember photos of Raymond wearing them.

After mama's visit it was not long before she sent a box to Grandmother. It contained a small baby doll. Grandmother took the doll and placed it in her kitchen on top of the icebox, saying "We will save this for Robbie." Robbie was not yet two years old and at the time she actually lived with Aunt Grace. Oh, how I loved the doll. I would pull up a chair in front of the icebox and sit and stare at the beautiful doll, knowing I was not allowed to touch. This went on for several days. I am in the straight back chair on my knees in front of the icebox doll just   looking at her. Grandmother comes over, takes the doll, and hands it to me. "Robbie is too small to even care about the doll. It's yours." I was thrilled.

Later the doll got me in trouble with Grandmother in ways that I did not understand. I was not yet eight years old; a young teenager, related to the family via some kind of marriage situation, came to Grandmother's home to play with me. We were in the yard, and she introduced the subject of where baby's come from. She explained to me about babies in our mother's bellies and how they might get out. I listened, as we played marbles and other dirt games.

However, that night, I took my sister's doll to bed with me. Assuming I had privacy under the covers that night, I took the doll and placed it between my legs above my knees, trying to imagine how a baby could come out of a woman's belly.

Suddenly my grandmother was at my bedside, jerking the sheet off me and exposing the doll I had placed between my legs. "What are you doing?" She exclaimed as she picked up the doll. I was more surprised at her interest than I was embarrassed. Looking at this event today, I did not have enough information to be embarrassed. I had no knowledge of sex stuff, nor that baby stuff was part of sex stuff; I was totally unaware of any adult protections set up to keep my innocence intact. This event was never spoken of between us.

CHAPTER THIRTEEN

Scrapbook History

(Interview with Olidia Ann Waters Carter)

The first time I ever saw the scrapbook I lived with Granny. I was between eleven and twelve years old. I did not just find it; she showed it to me.

I lived with Grandmother and my daddy, because my parents were separated. I could not get along with my mother at the time. Mama had a drinking problem. So, I went to live with my daddy, who was living at Grandmother's house. I don't remember exactly how long I lived there. I slept with my grandmother and my daddy slept in the other bedroom. I was maybe age eleven or twelve. We were there with her for a good while.

I did not know that she ever attended any kind of sewing classes until years later. The scrapbook came about as a result of Grannie taking sewing classes when she was younger, where she made the items that were in the scrapbook—different stitches and sewing techniques, like making sleeve cuffs. My grandmother was in her 70's when I lived with her. The scrapbook was hers from years ago. She had a wooden cabinet in her room where she stored bedspreads, rugs, and personal things. In the wintertime, instead of putting the rugs on the floor, she put them on her bed to keep her feet warm. I did not know how it came about that grand-mother made the scrapbook. Years later, I got the scrapbook from my stepmother, Sara. I can only speculate how she came to have it. Sara and Daddy were married when he died, and the scrapbook had to have been part of his property she had preserved as important.

I was grown and married and living in Hazlehurst, Georgia, maybe thirty miles from Alma. Sara's daughter lived in Hazlehurst, also. The daughter called me saying that Sara was ill and asked me to go with her to visit her mom.

At Sara's house, we were talking about missing my Daddy. I said something like I did not have any mementos that had been my grandmother's. Sara excused herself and came back into the room with the Scrapbook in hand. I knew it existed, but I had never seen it before, thinking it went missing when Daddy died. Sara presented it to me.

I had never given Grannie's sewing skills much attention. I took the scrapbook home with me and stuck it in a drawer. Yet, through the years traveling with a military husband to Texas, to Missouri, back to Georgia, I kept it safe. I have held on to it for years.

As a child, I didn't see any significance in it. But I did remember seeing the bonnet that was on the last page. It looked almost like a doll bonnet. It was cute and pretty. I do not have a clue what happened to it. It was missing when the scrapbook was given to me. But I had seen the bonnet when I was young.

Who do I think took the bonnet? Only a female relative would have taken it. I was told that my Aunt Pearl and Uncle R. H., while we were at Grandmother's funeral, went to Grannie's house and removed what they had given her in the past and whatever else they wanted.

I don't know how Sara, my stepmother, ended up with the scrapbook. There was also a set of cotton carding boards. Sara gave me those at the time she gave me the scrapbook. This was years after Grandmother's death.

My recollection of how Grandmother came to be crippled was she fell out of a wagon landing on some kind of garden stalk injuring her leg.

My granny did not like to let you wash dishes. And she was fussy about her bed. She had a feather-mattress and you did not go near that bed in the daytime. You didn't sit on the bed. You didn't lean on the bed, and you did not dare lie on the bed, like kids do today. You respected the bed.

This was around 1957. Granny Henderson was age 72 when she died. At the time she died, Daddy still lived there. That day, I had come home after working in tobacco for my uncle. I had taken a shower at mama's house that was right around the corner from Grandmother's house. After my shower, I went to Grannie's house.

Grannie had been sick. Aunt Grace and my daddy were there with her. Grannie was in her bed. I sat down on the side of the bed. She was trying to sit up in the bed. I kept saying, "No, Grannie, don't. Don't sit up."

She got about half-way up and fell over on me. I screamed, yelling for Daddy. He came running—he and Aunt Grace were in the kitchen trying to get her medication. Grannie died of a heart attack and fell over on me.

Daddy laid her back down. He told me to go move the truck; because he was calling the ambulance.

I was twelve years old. I rode with her to the hospital in the ambulance. I remember Daddy and Aunt Grace were behind us in her car. Daddy said she was dead before we left the house.

It was a hard time. That is why years ago when I got married, I was fine until nighttime. At night I was afraid to stay by myself, so my husband would take me to my sister's house. If they were not home, I would find somebody I knew to come and stay with me.

It took my husband going back into the military, and me having kids of my own, before I finally got over the fear of staying alone.

CHAPTER FOURTEEN

Death and Taxes

Granny died. Some years later Daddy died.

Looking back, is it possible that Daddy and Sara were not married; they just lived together? I come to this conclusion because after Daddy died,

Sara made no attempt to claim any of her husband's inheritance ownership of his mother's home; although, she continued to rent it out. I got involved because someone called to tell me the house was going to be sold at the Bacon County Courthouse for the past property taxes owed on it. Sara could have at least paid the taxes on the property from the rental income, but deliberately chose not to.

My sister Robbie and I attended the sale at the courthouse that day. Grandmother's house was not the only property going up for sale that day. There must have been eight to ten people in attendance in front of the courthouse. Word was passed around that Daddy's two daughters were there to buy the house. So, when the auctioneer described the property and opened the process for bidders, no one bid for the property but me. And my bid was just a few dollars above the taxes owed.

The house had never been completely finished, no real bathroom, just a commode and the kitchen was only a sink. I had $3,000 in cash. I gave this money to my sister Robbie, and she agreed to take on 45husband had recently died, and she used this job as part of her therapy of grieving.

I put no pressure on her, nor did I offer any suggestions about what I expected her to do. And I asked for no accounting of how she spent the $3.000. I trusted her completely.

She did a wonderful job. She finished the inside of the house, put in kitchen cabinets with a heating system, finished the bathroom, and painted everything that held paint inside and outside.

A few months later, she had turned it into a sweet little house. She never took any of the money to pay for her gas travel for the 30 miles from her home to Alma. Six months later her great grief over the death of her husband was healed, I had maybe $30 left over in the bank, the remodeled house was perfect—grand projects completed all around.

I rented it for some years, never really making any big money off it. I moved to South Carolina and decided at age 50 to become a college student. The money I received from the house rental, and later sale, went toward paying my college tuition. I am certain my grandmother, my daddy and my siblings were satisfied with my management and disposition of our grandmother's property.

Scrapbook

Even Basting

uneven Bast

Running Stit

construction
stitch

half
Backstitch

stitching
stitch

Flat Fell

Tucks

Plain

gausetted

whiped

Pin

Pleated

Gathered
Rufels

heated
Rufels

Pleat

inverted

hems

Kick pleat

Collar

Cuffs

Neck Placket Board

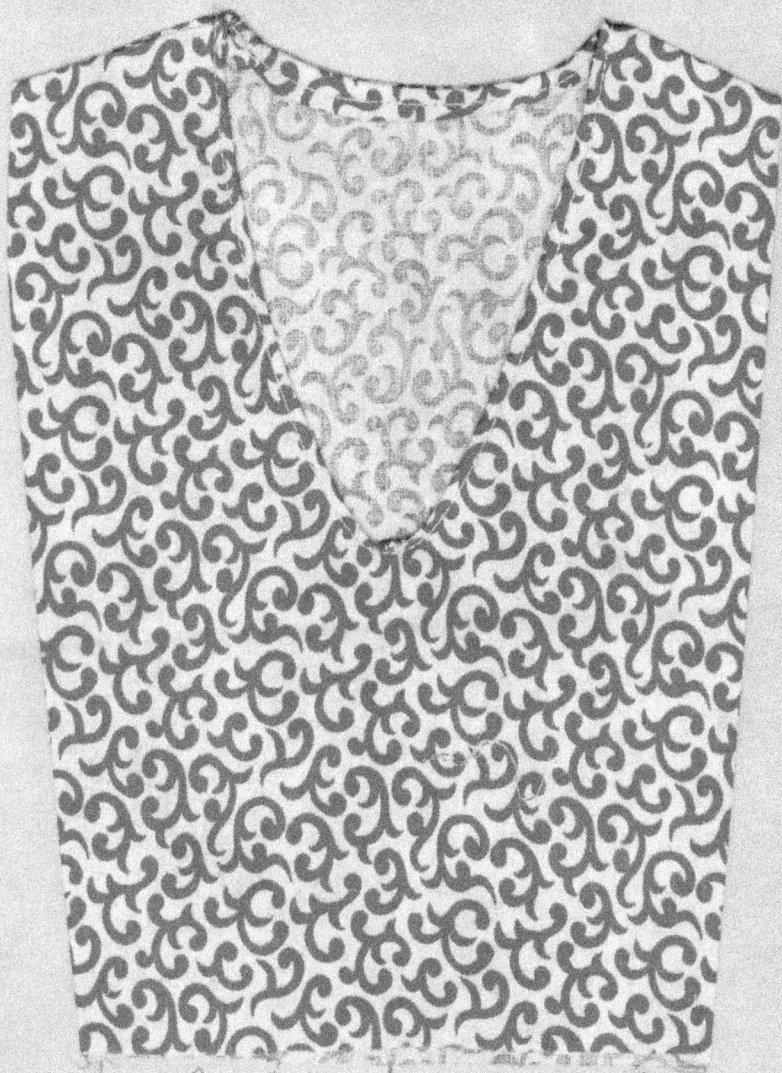

Bias facing V. neck

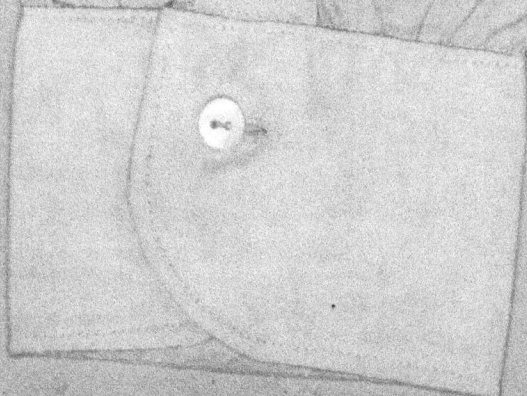

Shirt
Sleeve

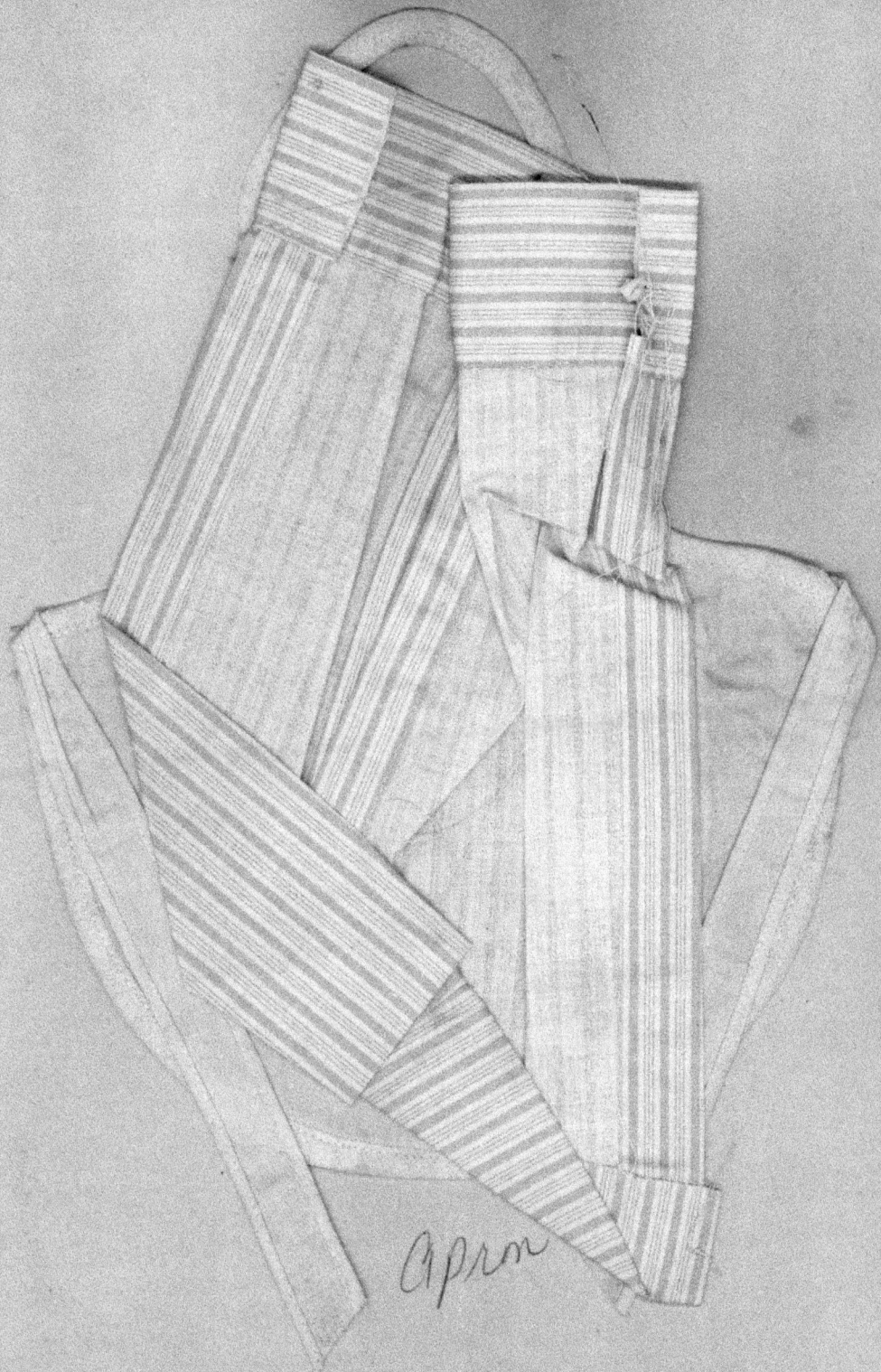

apron

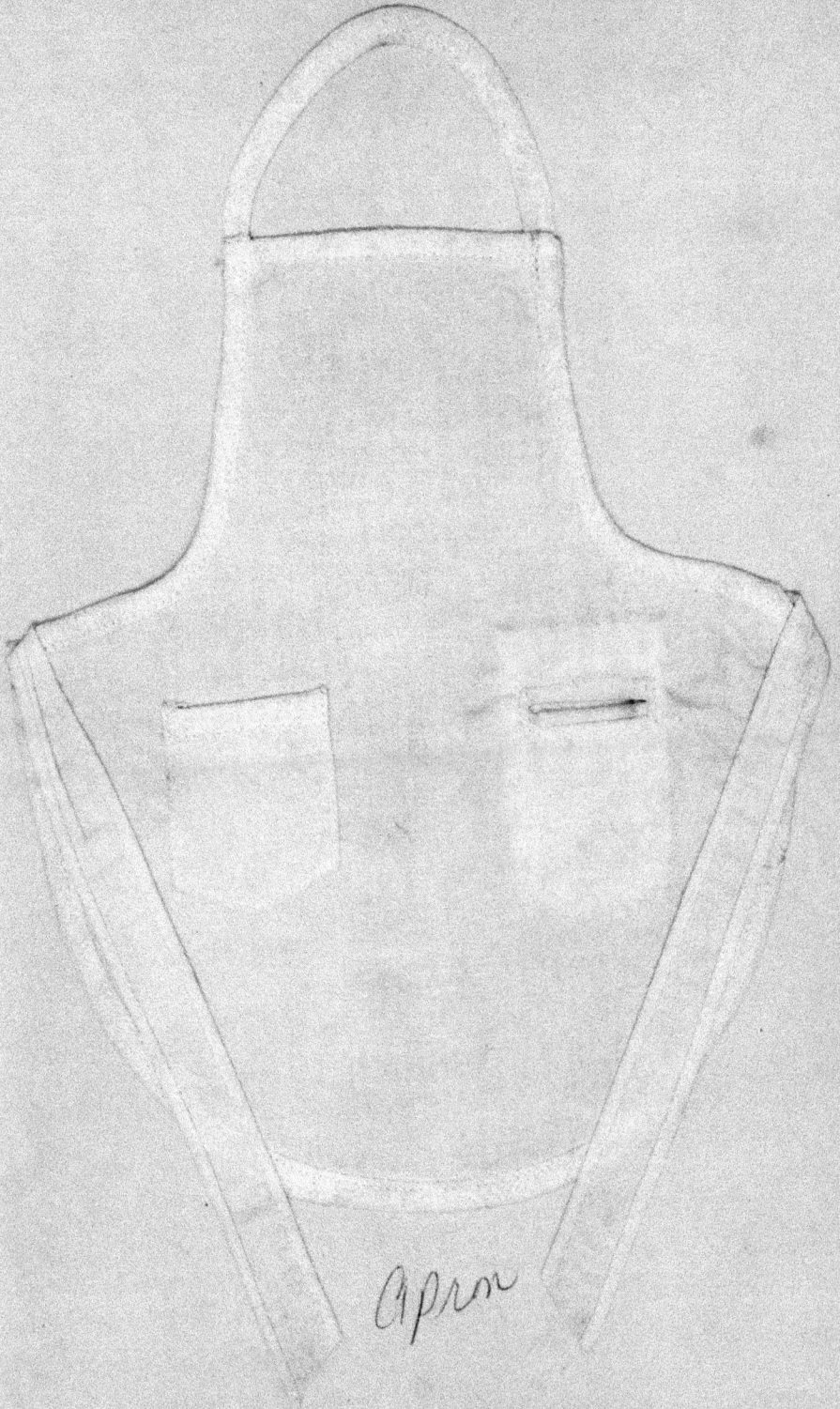

apron

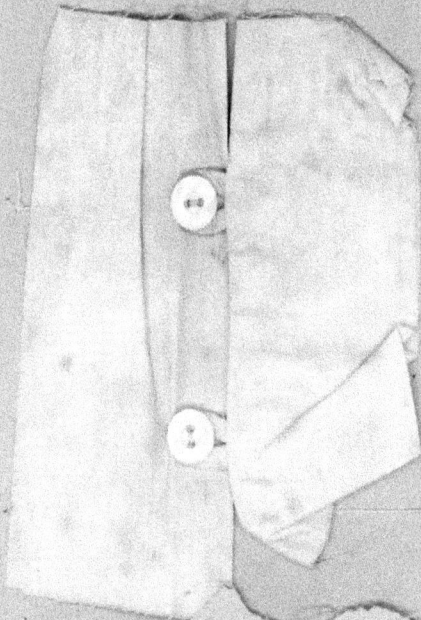

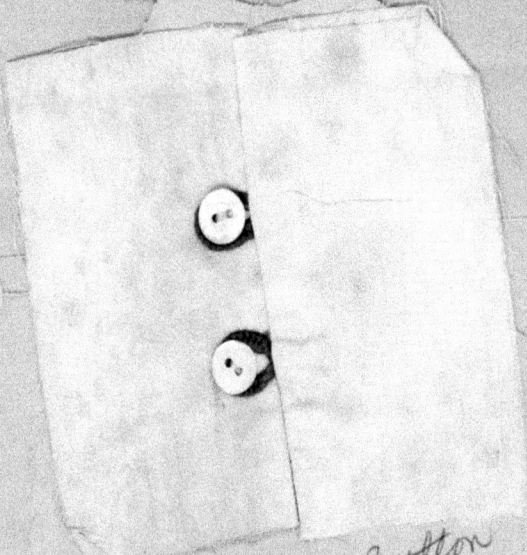

thread Loop Button holes

Chain Stitch

Out line Stitch

Briar Stitch

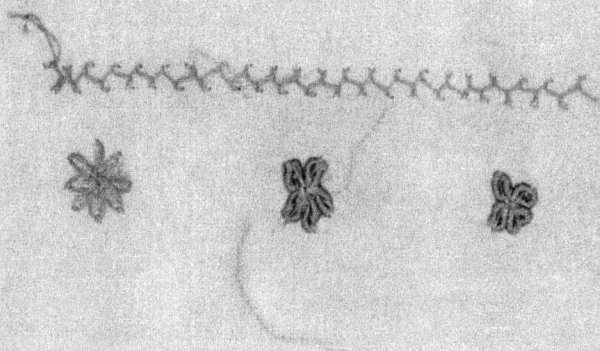

Wheat Stitch

him

Lazy Daisy

Smocking

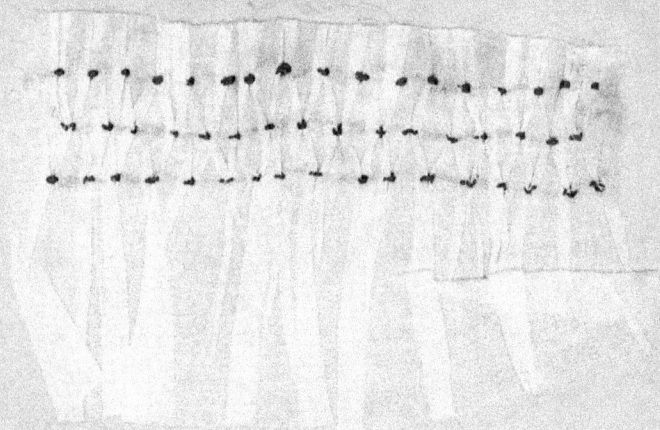

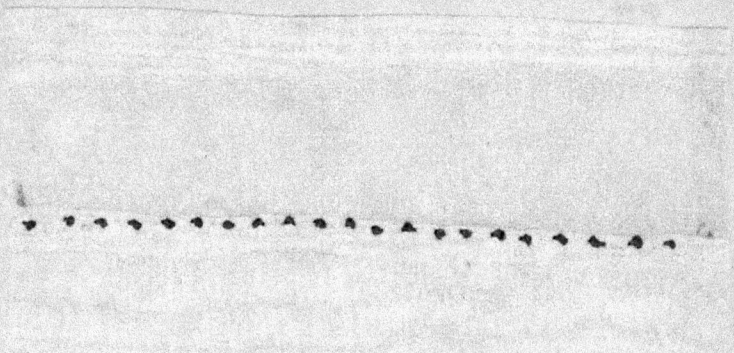

French Knots

String

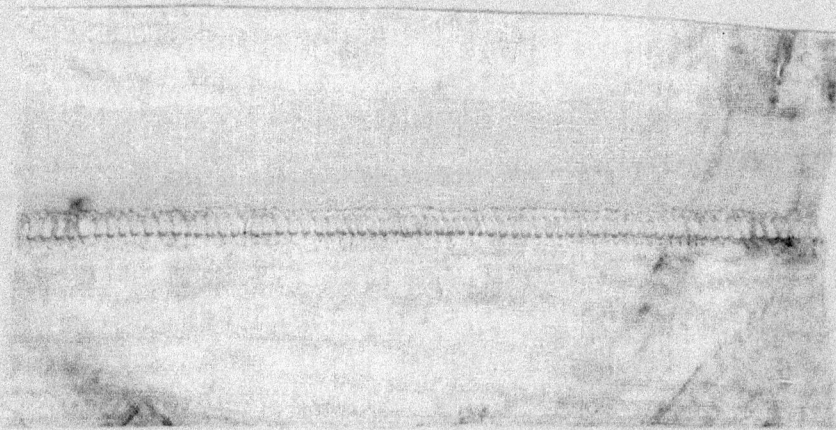

hem
stitching

hems

Smocking

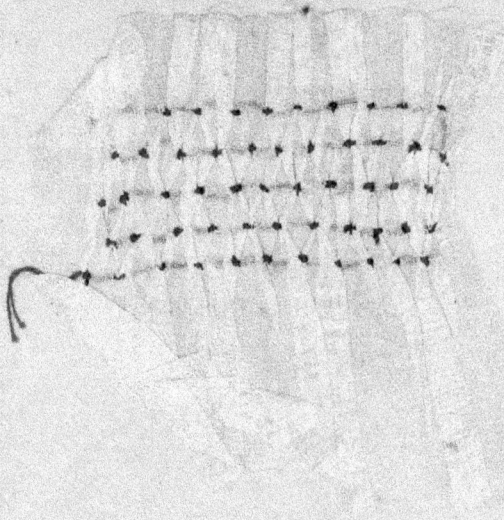

wheat stitch   french knots

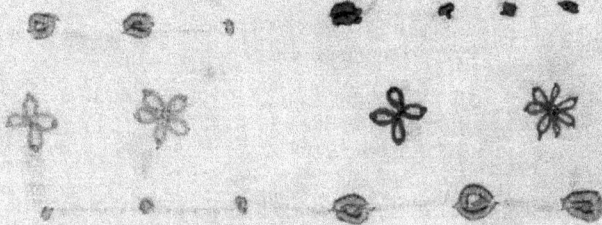

Lazy Daisy

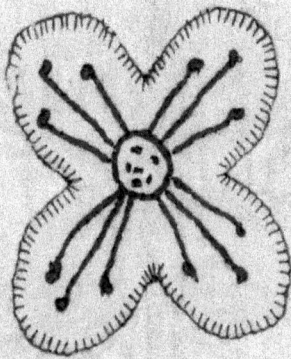

offbzz

Bound Button Holes

Barnerett

CPSIA information can be obtained
at www.ICGtesting.com
Printed in the USA
BVHW091256090222
628495BV00011B/1380